"Great men are like meteors," Napoleon Bonaparte once said. "They glitter and are consumed to enlighten the world." In February, 1815, Napoleon, whose career for nearly two decades was almost synonymous with the history of Europe, escaped from Elba, the tiny Mediterranean island to which less than a year before the allies had exiled him. Landing on the southern coast of France with a small force, he began the march to Paris. Thus began the Hundred Days, Napoleon's last reign as emperor of the French. While struggling with internal political problems, he endeavored to rally the French people once more and to convince them that he, rather than the Bourbon king, would best preserve the principles of the Revolution. Working with superhuman energy, Napoleon created a last army to face the allied forces under Wellington at Waterloo. The outcome of that battle and of the Hundred Days had a lasting effect on the political realities of Europe.

PRINCIPALS

NAPOLEON BONAPARTE, the former emperor of France whose escape from exile and return to France began the Hundred Days.

LOUIS XVIII, the kindhearted but imprudent Bourbon king who replaced Bonaparte on the throne of France and was forced to flee the country during the Hundred Days.

MICHEL NEY, Napoleon's most colorful marshal, the hero of the Russian campaign.

THE DUKE AND DUCHESS OF AGOULÊME, related to the Bourbon kings and strong royalists against Napoleon.

JOSEPH FOUCHÉ, Bonaparte's conniving minister of police, who began to plot against the emperor immediately upon Bonaparte's return.

ARTHUR WELLESLEY, Duke of Wellington, "the Iron Duke," whose army of British, Dutch, and Belgian troops faced Napoleon's Army of the North in the swift campaign that culminated at Waterloo.

PRINCE GEBHARD VON BLÜCHER, the vindictive seventy-two-year-old field marshal who commanded the Prussian army opposing Napoleon in Belgium.

EMMANUEL GROUCHY, the plodding, literal-minded marshal of Napoleon whose absence from the field at Waterloo had a crucial effect upon the outcome of the battle.

Napoleon Bonaparte at the time of the Hundred Days.
(United Press International)

THE HUNDRED DAYS ;

Napoleon Returns from Elba to Meet Defeat at Waterloo ₍

By John T. Foster

(A World Focus Book)

FRANKLIN WATTS, INC.
NEW YORK, 1972

For Jane Jones

Maps by George Buctel

SBN 531-02157-2
Copyright © 1972 by Franklin Watts, Inc.
Library of Congress Catalog Card Number: 71-184358
Printed in the United States of America
6   5   4   3   2   1

Contents

Escape 3

The Road to Elba 8

The Road Back 14

The Iron Cage 17

The Hundred Days Begin 19

Outlaw 21

Internal Troubles 23

Who Will Lead the Troops? 26

The Road to Brussels 28

The Gathering Tempest 31

Quatre Bras and Ligny 33

The Lost Twelve Hours 39

Waterloo 42

The Charge of the Imperial Guard 49

The End of the Hundred Days 54

Aftermath 58

Bibliography 61

Index 63

The Hundred Days

Napoleon with his men aboard the Inconstant *returning to France from his exile on Elba. (The Bettmann Archive)*

Escape

The night was dark and still. An open carriage came rumbling down the steep hill accompanied by a file of troops with the red, white, and blue cockade of revolutionary France in their bearskin shakos. As the carriage passed through the narrow streets of the town, the flickering oil lamps lighted up the pale, brooding face of its occupant. Townspeople cheered him lustily.

It was Sunday, February 26, 1815. Napoleon Bonaparte was escaping from Elba, the tiny Mediterranean island to which he had been exiled nearly a year earlier. The period known as the Hundred Days, one of the most dramatic in history, was about to begin.

Lights appeared in windows all over town. As the carriage and its honor guard neared the harbor, a boat crew waiting there began to sing the French patriotic hymn, the "Marseillaise." Wives of the soldiers and other civilians joined in.

> *"Allons, enfants de la patrie,*
> *Le jour de gloire est arrivé!"*
> Come, children of the homeland,
> The day of glory has arrived!

Napoleon and his men stepped into rowboats and were taken out to the waiting ships. The moon rose about 9:00 P.M. The emperor's little fleet, the sixteen-gun brig *Inconstant* and six smaller craft, remained at anchor until midnight when the wind came.

The crowds watching from shore once again broke into

cheers as the white sails filled out in the moonlight and the seven vessels began to glide down the gulf toward the open sea. Napoleon was embarked upon the last great adventure of his career.

Aboard the *Inconstant* with the emperor were four hundred troops of the Imperial Guard. Six hundred more were crammed into the other vessels. With such a force the audacious Napoleon proposed to invade France, march to Paris, and again take control of the nation.

In the night, the little fleet scattered to avoid detection, and the afternoon of the following day a warship overtook the *Inconstant*. She was discovered to be a French cruiser from Toulon. As daring as he was, Napoleon could not take the chance of testing whether her crew was loyal to him or to the Bourbon king, Louis XVIII, who then sat on the throne of France.

The brig cleared for action; the guns were shotted and run out. Then Napoleon ordered his guard to lie down on the deck so they would not be seen from the cruiser. As the bigger ship drew alongside, an officer on the *Inconstant* took up the speaking trumpet and shouted across the water, "Where are you bound for?"

"For Leghorn," answered a voice from the cruiser. "And you?"

"For Genoa," the officer lied. "Have you any messages?"

"No," the voice answered. "And how is the great man?"

"Wonderfully well," the officer on the brig replied. Napoleon was standing next to the officer, telling him what to say. The two ships drew apart, and Napoleon sailed on toward France.

"I shall be in Paris without firing a shot," he told his men. He knew he had to be. Any bloodshed would set off a civil war, which would mean his doom.

FRANCE
1815

ENGLAND

CHANNEL

ENGLISH

KM. OF THE NETHERLANDS

KINGDOM OF PRUSSIA

Brussels
Waterloo
Charleroi

Lille

LUXEMBOURG

PALATINATE

GRAND DUCHY OF BAVARIA

Metz

Strasbourg

Seine River

Paris ★

Fontainebleau

Loire River

Lons-le-Saunier

Saone River

SWISS
CONFEDERATION

F R A N C E

Rochefort

Lyons

Grenoble

KM. OF SARDINIA

BAY OF BISCAY

N

Bordeaux

Rhone River

Avignon

Cannes

Garonne R.

Marseilles

0   50   100   150
Miles

SPAIN

MEDITERRANEAN SEA

Tuesday morning those on the brig could see the jagged outline of the Alps far to the north. That night they sighted the bobbing lights of other ships approaching. Napoleon's little fleet was reassembling.

Wednesday, March 1, France came into view. That afternoon the fleet anchored near Cannes, in the Provence region, and began to unload men, horses, and equipment. Before nightfall, the emperor was standing once more on French soil.

There was no turning back now. Already Sir Neil Campbell, the British commissioner whose temporary absence from Elba had permitted Napoleon to escape, had returned and found his charge missing. The emperor knew that Sir Neil would waste no time in getting word of the escape to the mainland. Bonaparte marched north along the snowy mountain road toward Grenoble. There, he knew, was a critical test, for the town had a strong garrison under a royalist commander.

Rounding a bend in the road in the Laffray Pass the afternoon of March 6, Napoleon's small force encountered the Fifth Regiment of the Line drawn across their path with fixed bayonets. The troops wore the white cockade of the Bourbons in their shakos. The emperor dismounted and ordering his men to ground their muskets, walked toward the other troops. His short, broad-shouldered figure in the familiar green greatcoat immediately identified him. An officer of the king's men yelled an order to fire.

The order was not obeyed. The troops watched as if hypnotized as Napoleon walked closer, unbuttoning his coat and holding it open. He called out in a firm voice, "If there is one of you who would kill his Emperor, here I am!"

A single shot could have finished the venture at that moment, but no one fired. The only sounds were the officers' furious

Above, Napoleon at the head of his troops approaches the loyalist royal troops on the road near Grenoble. Right, Napoleon being welcomed by the citizens of Grenoble. (The Bettmann Archive)

commands, which the troops ignored. Then someone shouted, *"Vive l'Empereur!"* The cry was taken up until it thundered; men broke ranks and rushed forward to embrace Napoleon, to touch his hand, his sword. They tossed their shakos into the air, plucking out the white cockades.

Their actions made it clear that the rank and file of the king's army was for Napoleon. He had won the crucial first round. As he later said, "Before Grenoble, I was an adventurer; at Grenoble I was a reigning prince."

The Road to Elba

The phenomenal career of Napoleon Bonaparte had begun during the French Revolution. He came to the country's attention in 1795 when he showed great resolution in putting down an uprising in Paris against the government of the Directory. In command of a French army he carried on a successful campaign in Italy as part of the French effort to spread the revolution to other countries still ruled by monarchies.

Napoleon moved from the military to the political arena in 1799 when, by a coup d'état, he became head of the government of France as First Consul. He was thirty years old at the time. He began a series of governmental reforms, the most important of this period being the establishment of a new code of civil law, called the Code Napoléon. It enshrined the principles of the Revolution by establishing individual freedom in work, in conscience, and before the law. The Code Napoléon still forms the body of French law today, and the statutes of the State of Louisiana and the Province of Quebec are also based upon it. By securing a

Napoleon with Josephine, surrounded by his family and supporters, at the time of his selection as consul of France, in 1799.

The distribution of the eagles to the troops after Napoleon was crowned emperor in 1804.

broad-based internal government and setting up a national bank, Napoleon made enduring contributions to the strength of the French nation.

In 1804, at Notre Dame Cathedral in Paris, Napoleon had himself crowned emperor of the French, taking the crown into his own hands and placing it on his head himself. He defeated a coalition of European governments that fought against him; and he proceeded to remake the map of Europe, enlarging the borders of France and placing his relatives as rulers on the thrones of several countries. Within France, a dictatorship developed with tight political censorship, and the prisons were filled with political prisoners.

For the eleven years of Napoleon's reign almost constant warfare raged in Europe, in the colonies, and on the seas. During this period, Napoleon instituted the Continental blockade, intending to isolate Britain from European markets. But the blockade also had the effect of ruining the great cities of the Continent by curtailing European industries, especially the textile industry. This economic decline, together with the burdens of taxation and the requisition of troops needed to carry on the wars, led to increasing popular opposition within the Empire.

Perhaps unwittingly, by reshaping frontiers and imposing unity in such previously fragmented countries as Italy and Germany, Napoleon helped them along toward eventual independence as nation-states. His armies taught Europe nationalism. They dramatically demonstrated what a people in arms — bound by ties of language, culture, and history — could do. And they aroused a fierce national patriotism in opposition to that of the French.

Meanwhile the structure of the Empire was fragile, being

A contemporary political cartoon: "Napoleon throws sand into the eyes of the masses."

imposed from the outside and lacking support from intellectuals or politicians or — as the bloody years dragged on — from the majority of the French people.

It was Russia and her terrible winter that brought Napoleon to the beginning of his downward plunge. In 1812, the debacle of his invasion of that vast country, his last rival on the Continent, and the destruction of his Grand Army of six hundred thousand men, proved that Napoleon was not invincible. A new coalition formed against him, and Napoleon raised a second Grand Army — this one numbering four hundred and twenty thousand men and boys — almost all raw recruits. By the spring of 1813 every third male in France between the ages of seventeen and

11

The entry of Louis XVIII into Paris on May 3, 1814.

forty-three was in uniform. In the three-day Battle of the Nations at Leipzig, Germany, Napoleon's army was crushed.

Yet this incredible man raised still a third army, and an exhausted France was able to hold off the armed might of Europe for more than four months. The allies, however, could not be denied and closed in on Paris, which surrendered on March 30, 1814. On April 6, Napoleon abdicated. King Louis XVI had been guillotined in 1793. His brother was now placed on the throne of France as Louis XVIII.

By the Treaty of Paris, the allies permitted Napoleon to retain the title of emperor and gave him the sovereignty of the small island of Elba, off the coast of Italy, to which he was exiled.

He was to have an annual income of two million francs from the French nation.

Napoleon was anxious that his second wife, the Archduchess Marie-Louise of Austria, whom he had married in 1810 after divorcing Josephine, his first wife, should join him on Elba with their young son, Napoleon Francis, named the king of Rome by his father. But Marie-Louise's father, Francis of Austria, and his minister of foreign affairs, Prince Von Metternich, refused to let the archduchess and her son go with Napoleon. Under their pressure Marie-Louise later wrote to the Congress of Vienna, the conference held by the allies after the signing of the treaty, stating that she wished to have nothing more to do with her husband. Napoleon was never to see his wife or child again.

The emperor loved them and needed them as symbols of legitimacy and as a guarantee of succession to the throne. Their absence depressed him to the extreme. "Life," he told his confidant, General Armand de Caulaincourt, "has become intolerable."

He took poison from a vial he had carried in the retreat from Moscow, but it had lost its potency and merely made him sick. Napoleon never tried to commit suicide again.

On April 20, 1814, he set off for Elba escorted by four commissioners representing Great Britain, Russia, Austria, and Prussia. At Avignon in Provence, his carriage was stopped by an enraged royalist mob and he was nearly lynched.

Terrified, the emperor thereafter disguised himself as a postilion, riding through the rain and mud in front of his own carriage. Later he wore the various uniforms of the allies to escape the eyes of his countrymen. He breathed easily only when he boarded the British man-of-war H.M.S. *Undaunted*, and began the cruise to his island of exile.

13

The Road Back

Napoleon took possession of Elba on May 4, 1814, hoisting a new flag with the golden bees that were his personal insignia. The man who had ruled Europe from Spain to Poland was emperor of a tiny (eighty-six square miles) mountainous island between Corsica, where he had been born on August 15, 1769, and Italy, the scene of his first great military triumphs in 1796.

Yet Napoleon seemed to enjoy himself on Elba — at first. He explored his little domain thoroughly, riding tirelessly in the bright Mediterranean sun. Then he set up an administration and began to govern the one hundred and twelve thousand islanders, who took to him at once. He urged the seven hundred members of the Imperial Guard who had followed him into exile, and who did not already have wives, to marry. He began an extensive road and bridge construction program. He gave great attention to the planting of trees.

His mother and attractive sister, Pauline, arrived in July to keep him company. Napoleon amused himself by cheating them at cards and playing practical jokes on his Grand Marshal, Henri-Gratien Bertrand, such as slipping a fish into the marshal's pocket and then asking Bertrand to lend him his handkerchief.

Travelers began to include Elba on their itinerary. Napoleon received them, especially if they were distinguished Englishmen who could give him the news of Europe.

"Tell me frankly," the emperor said to one tourist late that year, "are the French happy?"

The traveler shrugged.

Napoleon answered himself. Of course the French weren't happy, he said. They had been too humiliated by the peace terms. England had forced a king on them, and they would never accept the loss of Belgium.

"You will live to see another war," Napoleon told one British visitor, "for Belgium."

This little country came up repeatedly in his conversations with foreign visitors, for he seemed to be obsessed with Belgium that winter. His own little domain was beginning to bore him, and news from France was most interesting.

The French people had reached a high pitch of patriotism during their struggle in the Revolution and during the following period when neighboring monarchies threatened their country. As the head of their government, Napoleon had brought stability to a chaotic situation, had led the French army to one victory after another, and then had established France as the center of a great empire. Although individual French citizens' liberties were curtailed under the empire, Napoleon at the same time was using newly developed techniques of propaganda to project in the minds of his countrymen a heroic image of himself and of France.

When Louis XVIII took the throne of France in 1814, it was as a constitutional monarch, his power being clearly limited by a new constitution. Among a number of influential classes in the country — new landowners, bourgeois industrialists and merchants, and civil servants — there was a strong fear of any return to the old-type Bourbon monarchy, which would disenfranchise them. Unfortunately for his new reign, Louis committed some unwise acts, such as reviving old court institutions, favoring exclusively his former companions in exile, and retaining certain restrictive excise duties.

These intimated threats of a return to old ways, working together with the damage to national prestige brought about by

15

the loss of imperial territory, developed in many French minds a dissatisfaction with Louis XVIII. Among the most anxious for a return to imperial glory were former troops of Napoleon's armies, three hundred thousand strong, who had been dismissed on half pay by the king.

The news from Vienna was at once encouraging and alarming to Bonaparte. First, the allies — still meeting at the Congress of Vienna — were squabbling about how the map of Europe should be redrawn now that France no longer controlled most of it. It was thought that the allies might go to war with each other any day. It was also rumored that the allies were considering the removal of Napoleon to a more remote spot, possibly to the bleak island of Saint Helena in the South Atlantic.

To make the emperor's situation even more uncomfortable, the Bourbons refused to forward him the two million francs revenue promised in the Treaty of Paris. He could neither pay his guard nor even maintain his meager household.

Such was Napoleon's desperate frame of mind when in February, 1815, a ship arrived from France. One of the crew came to visit the emperor. He turned out to be Fleury de Chaboulon, a fervent follower of Bonaparte, temporarily serving as a seaman in order to reach him.

There was a conspiracy, he whispered to Napoleon, among the northern garrisons to oust Louis from the throne and proclaim a Regency in the name of the emperor's son, the king of Rome.

"A Regency?" snapped the emperor. "Why a Regency? Am I dead?"

"Go, my son, fulfill your destiny," Napoleon's strong-willed mother urged. "You were not made to die on this island!"

16

Later — on another tiny island that was his death place — Napoleon confessed his ultimate motive for the escape from Elba and the invasion of France: "The fact is that what instigated me to return was the accusation of cowardice [during his journey into exile]. At last I could stand it no longer."

On February 16, Sir Neil Campbell, the British commissioner who was keeping guard on Boney, as the British called him, left Napoleon for a short visit to Italy. When Sir Neil returned on Febraury 18, he learned to his consternation that the bird, that most resolute of eagles, had flown the cage.

The Iron Cage

Of all the days of the week during the Hundred Days, Sunday plays the leading role. It was on a Sunday, as noted, that Napoleon escaped from Elba. Many of the other key events during this eventful period took place on what is usually considered the day of rest.

News of Bonaparte's invasion of France did not reach Paris until Sunday, March 5. Much of the emperor's success in his return was due to slow communications. France had an excellent signal system, a series of towers equipped with semaphores and called the telegraph. Using a telescope, a man stationed at one tower could read the message wigwagged from the preceding one several miles away, then pass it onto the next tower, so that a message could travel a long distance in a very short time. The telegraph did not begin until Lyons, however. By the time a courier reached that city with the fateful news, Napoleon was marching toward Grenoble.

About 1:00 P.M., shortly after the Sunday Court, the director of telegraphs came panting to the Tuileries with a sealed dispatch. He begged Louis XVIII's secretary to take it to the king personally.

Louis, grossly overweight, was suffering from an attack of gout in his hands and had great trouble opening the envelope. He read the contents, then put his huge head in his stiff hands.

"Do you know what this telegraph means?" he asked his secretary.

"No, Sire, I do not."

"Well, I will tell you," the king replied. "It is revolution once more. Bonaparte has landed on the coast of Provence."

The whirling arms of the telegraph flashed the news through France, causing confusion and mixed emotions. In the frontier fortress at Metz, Marshal Nicholas-Charles Oudinot, one of Napoleon's marshals who had declared his allegiance to the king after Bonaparte had abdicated the previous year, ordered his garrison to march to Paris. At Toul, 40 miles southwest of Metz, he set up temporary headquarters in a hotel and sent for his officers, who crowded into the room, forming a circle three men deep around him. It was night, and torches lighted the scene. Oudinot's wife Eugenie wrote down the incident for their children.

Oudinot addressed his officers: "Gentlemen, in the circumstances in which we now find ourselves, I appeal to your loyalty. . . . How would you and your men respond if I were to shout, 'Long live the King'?"

"Complete silence followed these words," Eugenie Oudinot wrote. "I never witnessed anything more striking. Hidden behind a curtain, I was compelled to watch this unique scene. . . ."

"Well, gentlemen?" the marshal demanded.

A young officer stepped forward and said, *"Monsieur le Maréchal,* yes, we must give an answer. No one here will contradict me. To your *'Vive le Roi'* the men and we ourselves will all reply *'Vive l'Empereur.'* "

"Thank you, sir," the marshal replied. He saluted them and they went out, one by one, without another word. Oudinot remained loyal to Louis XVIII and the Bourbons, but his men marched off to join the emperor.

Another more famous of Napoleon's marshals, Michel Ney, who also had sworn allegiance to the Bourbons after the emperor's abdication, stormed into the king's chambers.

"Sire," Ney is reported to have said, "if I take Bonaparte alive, I will bring him back in an iron cage."

He bowed to kiss the ring that Louis held out to him and immediately set off to arrest his former commander.

The Hundred Days Begin

Every hour brought more bad news to the royalists in Paris. Napoleon was marching north with ten thousand men. An entire garrison had gone over to him. Now Napoleon was marching north with fourteen thousand men. At inns where he stopped, the bones from his meals were saved as sacred relics. On March 16 the two chambers of the French legislature met in royal session to hear an address from the king.

"I do not fear for myself," Louis told them, "but I do fear for France."

The speech thrilled his listeners, especially the part where

19

he asked, "Could I, now in my sixtieth year, end my career in any better way than by dying for [France's] defense?"

On the evening of that same day came the news that Marshal Ney, in spite of his boast to the king, had gone over to Napoleon, taking six thousand troops with him. Clearly, Napoleon would soon be in Paris. Marshal Auguste Frederic Marmont urged the king to transform the Tuileries into a fortress that could be captured only after a long and bloody assault. Louis's heroism would arouse the enthusiastic support of France and all Europe, he said.

"Let Napoleon's last exploit be cutting the throat of an old man," Marmont went on. "Louis XVIII, by sacrificing his life, would win the only battle he had ever fought."

The proposal appealed to Louis. His ministers and court officials, however, who would be expected to play similar roles in the cataclysm, were less enthusiastic. They managed to persuade the aged monarch to drop the idea in favor of fleeing to Belgium.

The decision having been made, the necessity was to keep it as secret as possible. On Sunday, March 19, Napoleon was fifty miles from Paris. At noon that day the king reviewed the Royal House Guards as if everything was perfectly normal. But about midnight, while a raging rainstorm beat against the windows of the Tuileries, the door to the king's apartment opened. Behind a young page with a smoking torch, Louis XVIII appeared, leaning on the arms of two dukes.

The small crowd of royalists on the landing and the great staircase fell to their knees, weeping.

"I knew it would be this way," the king complained. Making his way down the stairs through the crowd with much difficulty, he said, "My children, I am touched by your loving concern. But I have need to harbor my strength. . . . Return to your homes. . . . I will see you again soon."

Outside, the rain was coming down in great, spattering sheets, drowning the torches. Louis was helped into the royal carriage, which sagged under his great bulk. It rumbled off into the night, followed by a troop of horsemen.

The Hundred Days had begun.

Outlaw

Next morning Paris saw that the white flag of the Bourbons was not flying over the Tuileries. The windows of the palace, usually crowded with soldiers, were empty. All was silence and gloom. The fact was clear: the king had fled.

Word quickly spread. People on the streets were tense, their faces somber, as they talked softly, glancing around them distrustfully. They acted as if they were on the verge of a catastrophe. In the shop windows, pictures of Louis began to vanish in favor of those of Napoleon. About noon the Bourbon flag came down from all the main buildings, and the Tricolor was raised as the city rang with shouts for Napoleon.

Paris was like a huge fair. Countrypeople and schoolchildren crowded the streets, carrying bunches of violets, Napoleon's flower. An army of workmen with scrub brushes and pails of soapy water moved through the city, cleaning uncomplimentary references to the emperor from its walls.

Hundreds of officers on half-pay crowded into the courtyard at the Tuileries in full uniform, embracing each other joyously.

21

In the throne room Napoleon's two sisters-in-law and their ladies-in-waiting, all in formal dress, were talking excitedly. Everywhere the fleur-de-lis, symbol of the Bourbons, had taken over from Napoleon's golden bees.

One of the women, staring down at the immense carpet that covered the throne room, noticed that one of the fleur-de-lis was loose. She ripped it off, revealing the imperial bees, and raised her trophy high. With squeals of delight, all the women in the room dropped to their knees, tearing away the fleurs-de-lis to make the carpet an imperial one again.

As evening came on, candles and torches flickered and flared in the palace. All over Paris church bells were clanging. The half-pay officers were packed to the point of suffocation in the entrance hall of the Tuileries and up the great staircase. Gradually the excitement built to the verge of being unbearable.

Shortly before 9:00 P.M. a distant roar came to the palace, growing steadily louder. Finally a carriage, escorted by a column of cheering mounted troops, pulled up outside. A short, square figure in a gray greatcoat alighted.

"Vive l'Empereur!" The ear-splitting shout was repeated again and again.

Napoleon was raised shoulder-high and carried through the hysterical mob past the entrance hall and up the staircase. His former postmaster general, Count Lavalette, a bulky person, forced a path, backing through the crowd, stammering, "It's you! It's you!"

The man addressed seemed to be oblivious to Lavalette's inane greeting and to all the excitement around him. On the emperor's pallid face, an eyewitness reported, was "the smile of

22

a sleepwalker." The short ride up the palace stairs was the climax of the long march from the beach at Provence to Paris — "the happiest period of my life," the emperor later called it.

As incredible as it seems, Napoleon Bonaparte had made good his proud prediction that he would reach Paris without firing a shot.

Internal Troubles

It would seem from Napoleon's spectacular march on Paris that France was solidly united behind him, but such was not the case. Louis XVIII had taken the throne of France as a constitutional monarch, and a certain portion of the population had confidence that he would protect their rights under the constitution. The king's strongest source of support, of course, was the French aristocracy. The land-owning upper class was naturally in favor of the king's rule, and there were rumors of a proposal to return some of the lands taken from the aristocracy during the Revolution. In addition, many of the old privileges of the nobility, such as exemption from military service, had been restored by the king.

Just a few moments before he fled the Tuileries, Louis XVIII gave Baron Eugène François de Vitrolles an order to go into the provinces and organize resistance to Napoleon there. At Bordeaux, Vitrolles joined forces with the Duke and Duchess of Angoulême, the son-in-law and the daughter of Louis XVI and Marie Antoinette and the nephew and niece of Louis XVIII. The duke and duchess had been in Bordeaux since March 5, to par-

23

ticipate in the celebration of the first anniversary of March 12. On that day the year before, in 1814, the city of Bordeaux had opened its gates to the Bourbons and the allies.

At the start of the week's festivities, the word came that Napoleon had landed in France and was marching on Paris. The duke was ordered to go and take command of royalist forces in the region of the Rhone River in southeastern France. He left Bordeaux on the night of March 9.

The duchess decided to remain in Bordeaux to rally royalist sentiment in the areas. There, however, as just about everywhere else in France, no matter how the civilians felt, the troops were for Napoleon. The arrival of Marshal Bertrand Clausel, sent by the emperor to take command of the region, brought matters to a head.

The duchess summoned the general in charge of the regular troops in Bordeaux and demanded point-blank whether the men would obey her. When he refused to give a direct answer, the duchess decided to go and find out for herself. Because of the danger involved, the general strongly advised her against this action.

"I am not compelling anyone to go with me," the duchess replied in her deep, masculine voice. "No more arguments . . . ."

She went to the barracks, where the troops had been confined in a surly mood. Her appeals met with shouts of support for Napoleon.

She stood haughtily, facing the demonstration until the men, impressed by her courage, grew silent. Only then did she withdraw, as drums beat a solemn salute to her bravery. Soon thereafter she took a ship for England.

"She's the only man in the family," was Napoleon's comment when he was told of the incident.

At the time, however, her husband was showing a marked degree of manhood that was surprising in a person of his puny appearance. The Duke of Angoulême established his headquarters at Nìmes in southeastern France, gathered four thousand men, and marched north. His royalist force repulsed Napoleon's troops, and captured Montélimar on March 30, entering Valence on April 3. But the emperor's columns began to move upon the royalists from three sides, and the counterattack fizzled out. The duke escaped to Spain, where he began to organize French royalist refugees to carry on the fight against Napoleon.

Vitrolles continued the royalist struggle at home. In mid-April, fifty thousand men in the western provinces rose up against the emperor. Napoleon finally was forced to send twenty thousand troops to put down the insurrection — troops he badly needed elsewhere.

In the meantime, the emperor was faced with treason within his own cabinet. He caught his minister of police, Joseph Fouché, conspiring with the Austrians against him. Before Napoleon's return, Fouché had been planning for the establishment of a regency for Napoleon's infant son, a regency in which Fouché would have had an important role. Fouché was a practiced opportunist who supported whichever side offered him the most power. In spite of his discovery, Napoleon could not afford to get rid of the influential Fouché.

As the contemporary writer and statesman, the Viscount de Chateaubriand, observed, Napoleon "had left France dumb and prostrate, he now found it standing up and talking back."

Fouché, meanwhile, went right on conspiring against the emperor. "He's very active right now," he remarked to an associate. "But he won't last three months. . . . I concede that he may win one or two battles, but he'll lose the third one, and that's when we shall have to go to work."

Who Will Lead the Troops?

One of the emperor's worst mistakes was to escape from Elba while the Congress of Vienna, meeting since October, 1814, was still in session. Communications being what they were then, it might have taken months for the allies to reach an agreement on what to do about Napoleon — time he could well have used in preparing his country for war. As it was — with Britain, Russia, Austria, and Prussia all represented at Vienna — they quickly settled their differences and pledged themselves to the destruction of Bonaparte, whom they branded an outlaw for having broken the Treaty of Paris.

A scene at a ball given by Prince Metternich during the Congress of Vienna. (The Bettmann Archive)

Their plan was for six armies, totaling more than five hundred thousand men, to cross the French border at various spots simultaneously about July 1, and march on Paris.

With all his old energy and brilliance, Napoleon rapidly gathered up an army to meet this host. He had two hundred thousand men under arms. He collected one hundred thousand more — many of them army deserters or men on extended leave. He also summoned one hundred and fifty thousand National Guards, and twenty-five thousand retired veterans accepted his invitation to rejoin the colors.

Less than half of these men would be combat troops. From the best of them he formed an elite military machine, as fine as ever fought under the Tricolor, which he called the Army of the North. There was an even more serious lack of materials than troops, however. Napoleon, working nearly around the clock, collected the necessary money, requisitioned thousands of horses, and set up workshops to make ammunition, uniforms, and weapons.

The emperor had great difficulty in finding a marshal to lead his men into battle. Some of his old marshals, like Oudinot, remained faithful to the Bourbons. Another, Joachim Murat, the king of Naples, was a brilliant cavalryman who had won many earlier battles for France. But, on May 3, he rashly attacked the Austrians in support of Napoleon and was routed. When he fled to France, the emperor refused even to see him.

Napoleon's former chief-of-staff, Louis Alexandre Berthier, exhausted mentally and physically from the long years of almost constant warfare, had either jumped or fallen to his death from a window at his home, on June 1. When the emperor heard the news he burst into tears. To replace him, Napoleon picked

Marshal Nicholas Soult, who had had no previous experience as a chief-of-staff.

Emmanuel de Grouchy was a good cavalry general, but completely inexperienced in independent command. Among the emperor's available choices was Marshal Ney, but he was now confused by his defection from Louis XVIII, and Napoleon distrusted his reliability as an independent commander. As the showdown with the allies drew closer day by day, the emperor was plagued by the vital question: Who will lead the troops?

The Road to Brussels

The allied armies were stretched in a mighty crescent from the North Sea to the Alps. Napoleon knew full well that their objective was Paris. If they could push him out of the capital, he would no longer be emperor but an outlaw in fact as well as in name.

Two courses of action lay open to him: (1) he could mass his troops and fight a defensive campaign or (2) he could attack the enemy, defeating the allied armies one by one before they could join forces.

The emperor, typically, chose the second and bolder plan. He was **aware** that he could not rely on the loyalty of the French people if the allies were permitted to invade their exhausted nation a second time in little more than a year. On the other hand, if he could achieve a smashing victory, he could return to Paris as a hero and again rally France behind him to deal with the other enemy forces.

Across the northern frontier in Belgium, was an army of British, Dutch, and Belgian troops under the Duke of Wellington.

28

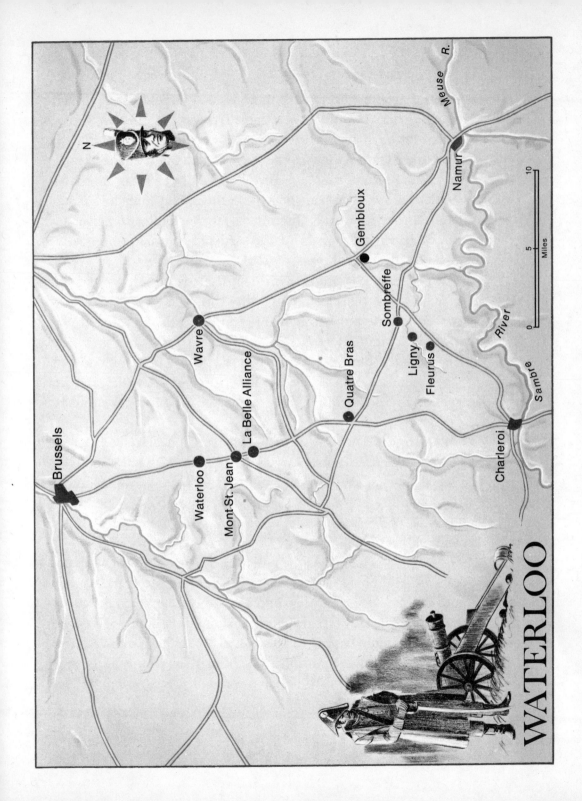

N

Meuse R.

Namur

10

Gembloux

Sombreffe

5

Miles

Ligny

Fleurus

River

Wavre

Quatre Bras

Sambre

Brussels

La Belle Alliance

Charleroi

Waterloo

Mont St. Jean

WATERLOO

Also in Belgium was a Prussian army led by Field Marshal Gebhard Blücher. Napoleon determined to attack the two forces, destroy them in turn, then dash to the capital at Brussels. He could then lay Belgium at the feet of his countrymen.

The shortest route to Brussels was by way of Mons or Charleroi. Mons had been heavily fortified, his scouts told Napoleon. So that route was discarded. To the southeast the heavy forest and rugged terrain of the Ardennes formed an effective barrier against a lightning attack.

The emperor studied his maps. Between Mons and the Ardennes was a gap of nearly thirty miles on either side of the town of Charleroi. Through this gap, the road to Brussels lay open by way of Quatre Bras and Waterloo.

Rapidly, brilliantly, Napoleon drew up plans for the campaign, sending the Army of the North toward the Belgian frontier in widely dispersed columns to disguise the ultimate goal.

Meanwhile he was forced to give a great deal of his attention to civil matters. After nearly a year of constitutional monarchy, France was a much different country from the one Napoleon had left. Upon his return from Elba, Colonel François La Bedoyère, one of Napoleon's former aides-de-camp, told the emperor, "You can no longer reign in France except on liberal principles."

Napoleon had ruled the nation as a dictator after he became emperor. But now he harkened to the new temper of the country and had a revision written into the Constitution, guaranteeing the people's civil liberty. He hoped to convince the French people that he was more willing to preserve the principles of the Revolution than were the Bourbons. On June 1, he swore an oath of fealty to the new Constitution at a ceremony, the *Champ de Mai.*

About forty-five thousand soldiers stood at attention and two hundred thousand spectators looked on at the last great ceremony of the Napoleonic era. Six hundred cannon boomed salutes as Napoleon, dressed in pink velvet knee breeches, silk stockings, and a hat decorated with plumes, rode up in a carriage drawn by eight horses. Perhaps the emperor had chosen the court dress to emphasize a desire for peace to the people of Europe, who had had nothing but war for a quarter century. Napoleon was a soldier, however, and not a dandy; in the court costume he looked rather out of place.

The ceremony, in which a High Mass was sung and the emperor distributed the eagle standards to his regiments, was an impressive one and apparently favorable to him. Yet only a week later, when the chambers met, the Chamber of Deputies elected as president not the emperor's choice, his brother Lucien Bonaparte, but Count Jean-Denis Lanjuinais, a man highly objectionable to Napoleon because he was firmly republican.

Angrily, the emperor warned the chambers, "Let us not imitate the example of the later Roman Empire which, invaded on all sides by the barbarians, made itself the laughing-stock of posterity by discussing abstract questions when the battering rams were breaking down the city gates."

On Sunday, June 11, Napoleon left for the Belgian front.

The Gathering Tempest

The emperor's Army of the North numbered one hundred and twenty thousand men. Opposing them were the Duke of Wellington's one hundred thousand British, Dutch, and Belgian troops

31

Arthur Wellesley, Duke of Wellington.

with headquarters at Brussels, and one hundred and sixteen thousand Prussians under Marshal Blücher with headquarters at Namur. The allied front extended about 90 miles, with its center at Charleroi.

One day shortly before the campaign began, Wellington was strolling in a Brussels park. An English civilian asked him how he thought he would do in the impending action. The duke pointed to a British soldier who had just entered the park and was admiring the statues.

"There," Wellington said, "it all depends upon that article whether we do the business or not. Give me enough of it, and I am sure."

The duke, however, did not have enough of that article to satisfy him. Only about one-third of his troops were British, and a great number had seen no combat. His hardened veterans of the Peninsular War were nearly all fighting in the United States in the War of 1812, and he sorely missed them.

32

He had "only thirty-five thousand men on whom I could thoroughly rely," Wellington said after the campaign. "The remainder were but too likely to run away." He hoped to solve his problem by mixing the troops he could rely upon with the undependable ones, so that the former would stiffen the backs of the latter.

In contrast, Napoleon's Army of the North was made up entirely of Frenchmen, almost all of them well-seasoned veterans in a frenzy of loyalty to the emperor. The army was extended between Lille and Metz, a distance of about 160 miles.

Napoleon moved quickly and secretly. French seaports were closed; coaches ceased to run; travelers were stopped at the border. By nightfall on June 14, the emperor had concentrated his army on a front less than 20 miles long directly across the frontier from Charleroi.

At dawn Thursday, June 15, the Army of the North surged across the Sambre River into Belgium, achieving complete surprise.

Quatre Bras and Ligny

The Army of the North was divided into two wings with a reserve. The left wing faced Wellington's army, the right Blücher's. The reserve was centrally located, ready to strike on either side. Napoleon was in charge of the right wing; the left still lacked a commander. On the hot afternoon of June 15, the emperor was seated at a table outside an inn on the road to Ligny when Marshal Ney rode up to him. Napoleon suddenly informed Ney that he should take command of the left wing, the First and

Second Corps. He instructed Ney to attack the Anglo-Dutch army next day at Quatre Bras, while the right wing dealt with Blücher's Prussians, wherever they might be.

Wellington, in Brussels, learned of the French attack upon Charleroi about 3:00 P.M. the same day. He could not be sure, however, that the Charleroi maneuver was not a feint to divert attention from the main attack upon Mons. Somewhere behind the French lines, the best of his scouts, Colonel Colquhoun Grant, was seeking out the enemy intentions, and the duke counted heavily on his report. When the vital document came to head-quarters, however, one of the duke's foreign officers did not consider it important enough to pass on, so Wellington never received it.

That night, to maintain an appearance of composure, the duke attended the Duchess of Richmond's famous ball in Brussels. At the height of the festivities, as the muttering growl of distant cannon came to the ballroom, a courier rushed in with a dispatch for Wellington: French units had attacked the Prussians, who were retreating.

The word quickly spread through the ballroom. Officers in the midst of a dance kissed the hand of their partners and rushed off to join their regiments. A bugle call split the night. Then from every quarter of the city, it was repeated. Drums began to beat and bagpipes started their wild skirl. In the streets, the steady thud of footsteps sounded as columns of troops assembled, along with the rumble of wagons and guns and the clatter of horses' hooves. Over all was the insistent blare of the bugles.

The men assembled with three days' provisions in their knapsacks. Many had wives and children who had followed them over from England. "One poor fellow," an eyewitness, Charlotte

Waldie, wrote, "immediately under our windows, turned back again and again to bid his wife farewell, and take his baby once more in his arms; and I saw him hastily brush away a tear with the sleeve of his coat, as he gave her back the child for the last time, wrung her hand, and ran off to join his company . . . ."

The Duke of Wellington remained at the Duchess of Richmond's ball, cheerful and charming but constantly interrupting conversations to send off dispatches to his generals. Then about 3:00 A.M. on June 16, he thanked his hostess and rode off to join his troops in the mellow light of a waxing moon.

Napoleon's orders of the day for June 16 clearly show that the emperor underestimated the strength of both Wellington and Blücher. Accurate reconnaissance has always played a crucial role in the tactics of a campaign, and a general is dependent upon the eyes of scouts, but they may not always see as sharply as he would himself.

It was not until about noon that Napoleon realized that the Prussians were concentrating at Ligny. He sent an order to Ney to attack the Anglo-Dutch before him, throw them back, and then join the right wing in utterly destroying the Prussians.

"In three hours the fate of the campaign will be decided," the emperor said. "If Ney carries out his orders thoroughly, not a man or gun of this army in front of us will get away."

The problem was that Ney's force, forty-six thousand men, was still marching up to the marshal. The Second Corps arrived before Quatre Bras about 1:30 P.M. The First Corps, with twenty thousand bayonets, was still coming up. Eager, as always, to begin the action, Ney started the assault, reasoning that the First Corps would rush up at the sound of the guns.

35

Napoleon on the heights at Ligny.

The French artillery opened fire at 2:00 P.M., and Ney led his men forward through a field of high corn. Suddenly three brigades of British troops arose from their hiding place in the corn and gave the French a withering volley of musket fire at close range, throwing them back.

At first outnumbered, Wellington's men were steadily receiving reinforcements, and Ney was in serious trouble. He kept searching the terrain behind him for his First Corps, whose twenty thousand bayonets could mean victory.

A courier from the imperial staff galloped up to the marshal, reporting that Napoleon had ordered the First Corps to attack the Prussians. A second courier arrived with another message from the emperor ordering Ney to fall upon the Prussians' right flank and rear.

"That army is lost if you act vigorously," this order said. "The fate of France is in your hands."

Ney was furious. To take away nearly half his forces at such a time obviously indicated that the emperor did not know about his desperate situation. With the First Corps — and only with the First Corps — he could drive the Anglo-Dutch army back, swing southeast, and smash the Prussians as ordered.

Marshal Ney sent a messenger to bring the First Corps back at once. In the heat of the fighting it did not occur to him that the First Corps could not arrive in time to do him any good; for it was then late in the afternoon, and night would bring an end to the battle.

The First Corps marched back and forth between the two battlefields, taking no part in either action, when its presence at one or the other probably would have meant a French victory. Wellington's casualties were about forty-eight hundred, Ney's slightly less. The English, Dutch, and Belgians stood fast.

At Ligny there was hand-to-hand fighting amid the blinding white smoke of burning thatch roofs. Frenchmen smashed cottage doors with their musket butts while Germans fired down at them from upper windows. With just enough daylight left for a final assault, Napoleon prepared to slam the Imperial Guard like a sledge hammer into the weakened Prussian center. The French artillery opened fire to prepare for the assault. But then overhead, as if in answer to the French cannonade, the skies thundered, and rain — the first of the campaign — poured down.

In the gathering gloom Blücher, ever a cavalryman, even at the age of seventy-two, led his hussars in a wild charge. The Prussian cavalry could make small impression upon the French infantry, who quickly formed squares that bristled wih bayonets and spouted fire which emptied the enemy saddles. Blücher's gray charger was shot and fell, rolling on the field marshal.

Badly bruised and semiconscious, the tough old warrior was led off the field. His army retreated north.

French casualties for the battle were about twelve thousand. The Prussians lost nearly sixteen thousand, as well as twenty-one guns. Also, another eight thousand men, who had come from provinces formerly in the French empire, deserted to Napoleon. The rain fell in torrents all night long. It fell upon the three armies, upon the wounded, the dying, and the dead on both battlefields — and upon the wives and friends who tirelessly searched with lanterns for their men.

Shortly after dawn on June 17, a courier, his horse flecked with foam, galloped up to the Duke of Wellington at his headquarters at Quatre Bras. The messenger leaned down and whispered into the duke's ear. Wellington's expression did not change. He gave the courier an order, then turned to his officers.

"Old Blücher has had a damned good licking and gone back to Wavre, eighteen miles," he said. "As he has gone back, we must go too. I suppose in England they will say we have been licked. I can't help it. As they are gone back, we must go too."

Soon thereafter a Prussian officer sent by Blücher arrived at Quatre Bras to learn Wellington's plans.

"I still hold to the original intention of a united offensive against the French Army," the duke replied calmly. "But I must now get back to the position at Mont St. Jean, where I will accept battle with Napoleon if I am supported by one Prussian corps."

In his new position before the little town of Waterloo, Wellington would be heavily outnumbered, and he desperately needed that thirty-thousand-man Prussian corps. Blücher's officer galloped off on a fresh horse to pass on the English general's reply, as the Anglo-Dutch army slipped out of Quatre Bras, heading for Mont St. Jean and everlasting glory.

The Lost Twelve Hours

Although Quatre Bras had been a stand-off and Ligny an indecisive win, Napoleon's opportunities for total victory were still tremendous. He could either pursue and destroy the Prussians or he could join Ney and crush the Anglo-Dutch army. Between 9:00 P.M. on June 16, and 9:00 A.M. on June 17, however, the emperor did nothing. In those vital twelve hours he lost the initiative and the campaign.

Shortly after 7:00 A.M. on June 17, following a good night's sleep, Napoleon climbed into a carriage to inspect the field at Ligny. He had grown quite fat during his stay at Elba, his "island of repose," as he had called it. The emperor's stoutness, his dull white complexion, and his heavy walk showed that he had lost much of the vigor of his early days. He rode much less than in the past and preferred a carriage to a horse.

As Napoleon was about to depart, Marshal Grouchy trotted his mount up to the carriage to ask for orders.

"I will give you orders when I judge it to be convenient," the emperor replied testily, and the carriage rumbled off.

Near Ligny, he got out and mounted his mare, Desirée. After several leisurely hours spent riding and in brilliant conversation with his officers about everything but the campaign in which he was involved, Napoleon finally took action.

He ordered two divisions and the Imperial Guard to Quatre

39

Bras. He sent Ney a dispatch ordering him to attack the Anglo-Dutch as soon as he was reinforced. Also, the emperor finally gave Grouchy his orders: the marshal was to take thirty-three thousand men and pursue the retreating Prussians to the east and prevent them from joining Wellington's army. (Actually the Prussians were headed north, as noted, toward Wavre.)

About 1:00 P.M., Napoleon appeared at Ney's headquarters before Quatre Bras. Having learned from a prisoner belonging to the rear guard that Wellington had evacuated, the emperor exclaimed, "France is lost!"

He had some sharp comments to make about Ney's failure to attack earlier. Ney retorted just as sharply that he had been merely following His Majesty's orders and was waiting to launch his assault when reinforced.

There was still time to make amends, however. Napoleon ordered an all-out pursuit of the Anglo-Dutch army; but another thunderstorm burst over the Belgian countryside, and the enraged French were bogged down. As in the Russian campaign weather was proving to be one of Napoleon Bonaparte's worst enemies.

Wellington's troops, with an earlier start, escaped to Mont St. Jean. Here the duke would stand and fight to the end, he and Napoleon meeting for the first time in their long careers.

At British headquarters, in a little inn at Waterloo that evening, Lord Uxbridge, Wellington's second-in-command, asked the duke what his plan was.

"Who will attack the first tomorrow, I or Bonaparte?" Wellington asked in return.

"Bonaparte."

"Well, Bonaparte has not given me any idea of his projects," the duke replied. "And, as my plans will depend on his, how can you expect me to tell you what mine are?"

Uxbridge bowed. His superior arose, laying a hand upon his shoulder.

"There is one thing certain, Uxbridge," he said. "That is, whatever happens, you and I will do our duty."

Wellington could not be sure that Bonaparte would attack him at Mont St. Jean. Napoleon might make a series of feints there, while preparing to launch his main assault at Hal, about 7 miles west of Waterloo, to cut off the escape route of the Anglo-Dutch army.

This is what the duke would have done if he had been in Bonaparte's boots — and which Napoleon probably would have done a few years earlier, before he became enamored of the frontal assault. In any case, to guard against such a possibility, Wellington sent seventeen thousand men and thirty guns to Hal.

That night Louis XVIII and his court were at Ghent, about 45 miles northwest of Waterloo. At the dire news of the Prussian retreat and the withdrawal of the Anglo-Dutch army, the Belgian city was on the verge of panic. But the king, fat and old, but brave, remained calm.

"Let those who are afraid depart," he said. "For myself, I shall not leave here unless forced to do so by the march of events!"

South of Waterloo the bivouac fires of the French and the Anglo-Dutch armies flickered on opposite sides of the parallel plateaus of La Belle Alliance and Mont St. Jean. About 1:00 A.M., on June 18, the dark skies poured down rain once more.

The wretched troops on both sides of the valley wrapped themselves in their cloaks and huddled together, trying to sleep.

41

Most of them succeeded: it had been a long, hard day. For many, it was their last sleep on earth as the slow, sodden hours brought them ever closer to one of the most celebrated battles in history.

Waterloo

The relentless Belgian rain was still falling steadily at dawn on Sunday, June 18, 1815. The two plateaus and the narrow valley between them were a giant bog, filled with puddles the size of ponds. Mud dripped like thick rain from the bellies of the horses; wagons and cannon were sunk to their axles in some spots, their crews struggling in vain with the slippery wheels.

Up since 5:00 A.M. at his headquarters in a farmhouse on La Belle Alliance, the emperor was pacing back and forth, taking repeated pinches of snuff, eager to start the battle. But his artillery commanders urged him to hold off until the rain had stopped and the sun had dried the ground, so they could maneuver their pieces.

As the French novelist Victor Hugo pointed out in *Les Miserables,* Napoleon "had a habit of holding all his artillery in hand like a pistol, aiming now at one point, anon at another. . . ."

The emperor himself said, "After the combat has started, he that has the skill to bring sudden, unexpected concentrations of artillery to bear upon a selected point is sure to capture it." But to aim cannon like pistols requires firm ground. "Captain Cannon" gave in to his artillery commanders and bided his time.

Still in high spirits, Napoleon had breakfast with his generals. When the silverware had been taken away, he spread his maps upon the breakfast table, chuckling, "Pretty checkerboard!"

He turned to his generals: "The enemy is twenty-five percent stronger than we are," he remarked. "Nevertheless, we have ninety chances in a hundred in our favor."

"No doubt, Sire, if Wellington were simple enough to wait for you," Ney answered. "But I can tell you that there are already marked signs of a retreat, and if you do not attack at once, the enemy will escape you."

"You have not seen rightly," the emperor replied, still smiling. "The time of retreat is over. Wellington would only expose himself to certain loss. He has thrown the dice, and they are for us."

In an earlier reconnaissance that morning, Ney had spotted allied troops climbing the slope to Mont St. Jean, and he had assumed that they were retreating. Actually they had bivouacked in the valley during the night and were merely going into their battle positions. When he spoke for an immediate assault, however, Ney was using good judgment. One of his superior's axioms backed him up.

"Loss of time in warfare cannot be made good," the emperor once said. "The excuses offered are always bad, for delays alone are the cause of the failure of operations."

When Napoleon said the enemy was 25 percent stronger than his forces, incidentally, he was mistaken. The troops that Wellington had dispatched to Hal gave the duke only 67,000 men, supported by 156 guns. Also, no matter how skillfully he might arrange them, 42,000 of these troops were Dutch and Belgian, with all the confusion of the language differences involved. Opposing his polyglot army, the emperor had 74,000 veteran, loyal Frenchmen, along with an overwhelming 260 guns.

Napoleon had received word from Marshal Grouchy of

Blücher's southwestward advance. The emperor planned to smash Wellington in a frontal attack before the Prussians entered the battlefield.

One of Napoleon's generals reported that the day before, he had eaten dinner at the inn where Wellington had had breakfast. The waiter told him, the general said, that one of the duke's aides had mentioned a junction of the British and Prussian forces south of Brussels. The emperor brushed the report aside: "After a battle like Ligny," he said, "that junction is out of the question for at least another two days. Besides, the Prussians have Grouchy on their track."

Marshal Soult, who had fought Wellington in the Peninsular War (winning high marks from the English for his fighting ability), was well aware of the British pluck and the accuracy of their musket fire. He urged the emperor to recall at least some of Grouchy's force to support the assault on Mont St. Jean.

The emperor's good humor vanished: "Because you have been beaten by Wellington, you think him a great general," he said sharply. "Well, I tell you, Wellington is a bad general, and the English are poor troops, and this will be a mere breakfast for us."

"I hope so, Sire," Soult replied evenly.

Napoleon's refusal to call back any of Grouchy's force and the plodding marshal's strict adherence to orders meant that he would not participate in the Battle of Waterloo. As at Quatre Bras and Ligny two days earlier, a powerful unit that could have meant victory for the French took no part in the action.

Outside, the Second Corps was marching past in the rain, and its commander, General H. C. de Reille, came into the farmhouse to report. What, Napoleon asked, did the Count de Reille think of the British? De Reille was another veteran of the Peninsular War. In a strong position, he replied, the British were unbeatable because of their grit and fire power. However, he continued, "the English are less agile, less flexible, less good at maneuvering than we are. If one can't defeat them by a direct attack, you can always do it by manuevering."

Napoleon shook his head. Waterloo would be a frontal assault — the bloodiest of battles. The day then was clearing, and the ground would soon be hard enough for him to move his guns. "If . . . [his officers] carry out my orders properly," the emperor said, "we sleep in Brussels tonight."

After ordering a leg of mutton for the victory dinner, Napoleon left the farmhouse. He sat motionless on his horse atop LaBelle Alliance as the Army of the North passed in review.

Blücher's march to Waterloo.

The bands played the "Marseillaise" and the eagle standards dipped before him as column after column of cheering men marched smartly past to the rattle of drums. Across the valley Wellington's troops waited quietly.

At 11:30 A.M. Napoleon launched his first attack. About an hour later the emperor, sweeping his glass around the horizon, sighted a dark mass on his right some 4 miles away. A grove of trees? A cloud shadow? Grouchy's column? It was actually a body of Prussian soldiers, the vanguard of the troops that Blücher had pledged to Wellington. The emperor determined to race time, to crush the Anglo-Dutch army before the Prussians could come to Wellington's relief. All during the hot June afternoon, the French columns were hurled against the Anglo-Dutch squares which stood fast.

The sound of cannon, the sputtering crash of musket volleys, the bursting of shells, the shouts of men, and the screams of horses made a deafening clamor. The galloping horses — mounted and riderless — and the great clouds of gray smoke, shot through with flashes of gunfire, multiplied the confusion. In a temporary lull, the colonel commanding the British artillery told the Duke of Wellington that he had the exact range of the spot where Napoleon and his staff were watching the battle on La Belle Alliance. "If Your Grace will allow me," the colonel said, "I think I can pick some of them off."

"No, no," the duke replied. "Generals-in-Chief have something else to do in a great battle besides firing at each other."

About 1:30 P.M. the emperor sent Ney against the Anglo-Dutch center at the head of four divisions, twenty thousand bayonets. They came on, plowed by British cannonballs, clawed by British grape and canister. Then Lord Uxbridge launched the

The charge of the Scots Greys at Waterloo.

British cavalry. Bugles sounding the charge, the Scots Greys crashed into the enemy before they could form square, throwing them down the muddy slope in great disorder.

"Scotland forever!" the horsemen shouted, charging headlong at the French guns, their magnificent dapple-gray horses throwing up thick clods of turf. They were joined by the Life Guards, the Royal Horse Guard Blues, and the Dragoon Guards. The British horsemen spiked thirty cannon and captured two French standards as well as three thousand prisoners.

But then the French cavalry hit them in overwhelming numbers when their own horses were blown by the furious ride. The ground trembled, thundering with the hoofbeat of thousands upon thousands of mounts, and horses reared, screaming, stamping around in circles as their riders hacked at each other with clanging sabers or slipped in the silent lance.

47

Of twenty-five hundred British mounted troops who charged down into the valley and up the slope of La Belle Alliance, fifteen hundred returned. Time, however, was running out for the French. Every minute brought the Prussian relief column closer to Mont St. Jean.

It was 3:30 P.M. Through the swirling smoke, Ney spied some wagons pulling back from the British line. They were actually just carrying off wounded, but Ney thought they marked the beginning of the British retreat. For the next two hours he launched a series of cavalry charges, leading most of them in person, having five horses shot out from under him that day. Dragoons, lancers, hussars, cuirassiers raced thumping down the hill, across the valley, and up the hostile slope into the murderous volleys of cannon and musket fire.

"Form square and prepare to receive cavalry!" The sharp

The Battle of Waterloo. (United Press International)

command was repeated so many times that afternoon that it became monotonous. The exhausted Anglo-Dutch soldiers rushed into their hollow squares, forming triple rows — kneeling, crouching, and standing, ready to fire and then hold off the horsemen with the bristling hedge of cold steel.

"I shall never forget the strange sound our bullets made against the breastplates of the [cuirassiers]," wrote Ensign Rees Howell Gronow of the First Regiment of Foot Guards. It was like "the noise of a violent hail-storm beating against panes of glass."

The Anglo-Dutch squares held, but they were shrinking steadily, their interiors filled with wounded, dying and dead. Napoleon's gunners were pouring cannonballs and flocks of grapeshot into the tightly packed ranks. The thicket of bayonets could stop the French cavalrymen but was no defense against the remorseless enemy cannoneers.

Eighty British guns stood silent, crews dead, ammunition exhausted. The colors of the Thirtieth and the Seventy-Third Regiments were sent to the rear to escape capture. Apprehensive staff officers rushed up to Wellington, asking if he had new orders.

"There are no new orders," the duke shouted over the tumult of battle, "except to hold out to the last man!"

The Charge of the Imperial Guard

It was 6:30 P.M. Marshal Ney was bleary-eyed with gunsmoke, sweat, and exhaustion; but he could see the unmanned British guns, the meager cavalry, and the threadbare red line of infantry

49

opposing him. At this point the fate of France was truly in his hands. He dispatched his aide-de-camp, Colonel Heymes, to Napoleon to ask for some troops to make a final, decisive assault upon the weakened British center.

"Troops?" the emperor shouted. "Where do you suppose I shall find them? Do you expect me to *make* them?"

At the moment he was surrounded by fourteen full battalions of the Imperial Guard, enough to smash through the Anglo-Dutch center and bring resounding victory to the Tricolor. The most celebrated troops in the world had seen no action that day, although their bands had been very busy playing brave airs for those who were doing the fighting and the dying.

Napoleon once said, "Generals who withhold troops until the day after the battle are always beaten." Again he said, "When you wish to join battle, get all your forces together, neglecting none of them. Sometimes the day is decided by a single battalion."

But Napoleon Bonaparte, perhaps the greatest gambler in

The last square of the Imperial Guard at Waterloo.

history, had lost his nerve. "I felt that Fortune was deserting me," he said later of the Battle of Waterloo. "Not to venture means doing nothing at the favorable moment, and one never ventures without being convinced of one's Good Fortune."

At 7:30 P.M., the sun was sinking on the Battle of Waterloo, and the Prussians were flooding onto the field like the sea through a break in a dike. Napoleon was ill and had taken small part in the conduct of the battle, leaving it almost entirely in the hands of Ney, whose heart had always been stronger than his head. But, at last, the emperor stirred himself out of his lethargy and led five battalions of the Imperial Guard down the hill to Ney.

"To Brussels, my children!" Napoleon shouted as the Guard marched past. "To Brussels!"

Drums beating, bugles blaring, Marshal Ney in the lead, the Imperial Guard marched up the hill toward Wellington, who had used the delay to transfer troops from both flanks to strengthen his center. All British eyewitnesses were in agreement that if the attack had come earlier, when Ney first asked for reinforcements, it would have smashed the Anglo-Dutch center. As it was . . .

In four compact squares, their bearskin shakos making them look like giants, the Guard climbed the hill through a cornfield toward the heights of Mont St. Jean. Fifty British guns, double-charged with grape and round shot, belched fire.

"Now, Maitland, now's your time!" Wellington shouted. "Up, Guards, and at 'em!"

Sixty feet from the French, Sir Peregrine Maitland's Guards Division rose up from the corn, where the men had been lying in ambush, and delivered a devastating volley. Then they charged with the bayonet. As the two elite units fought hand-to-hand,

51

Wellington's Fifty-second Infantry Regiment crashed into the enemy flank. Ranks broken, the Imperial Guard poured in a torrent back down the slope.

"*La Garde recule!*" The awed cry resounded throughout the French army. "The Guard is retreating!" Then came an even more ominous cry: "*Sauve qui peut!*" Every man for himself!

The defeat of the Imperial Guard signaled the defeat of all their compatriots. The Army of the North was smashed into smithereens like a jug hurled against a rock. No more an army but a mob, the French broke into headlong flight. Napoleon Bonaparte's bright star, which had kept Europe ablaze for nearly twenty years, went spinning down in the Belgian twilight.

"Now it is all over," he murmured. "Let us get away."

Ney remained. Brandishing a broken sword, bareheaded, face blackened with gunsmoke and streaked with sweat, he still fought desperately to rally his men. "Come and see how a Marshal of France can die!" he roared, but the men did not pause in their flight.

Unwounded but on the verge of collapse from fatigue, Ney stumbled away on the arm of an Imperial Guardsman. He was the last senior French officer to leave the field.

In the action the French had lost more than two hundred cannon and one thousand vehicles. Their casualties were nearly forty thousand. Wellington lost about fifteen thousand, the Prussians seven thousand. So confined was the fighting that about forty-five thousand dead and wounded lay within a space of 3 square miles on the battlefield of Waterloo.

The day after the engagement Wellington wrote his brother William, "It was the most desperate business I ever was in; I never took so much trouble about any Battle, and never was so

52

The meeting of Wellington and Blücher after the Battle of Waterloo.

near being beat. . . ." Then the duke went on to sum up the reason for his victory: "Our loss is immense, particularly in that best of all instruments, British Infantry. I never saw the Infantry behave so well."

A few weeks later, this stiff, stern warrior, who had always seemed to revel in the smoke and din of mortal combat, revealed a well-guarded facet of his personality to a friend, Frances, Lady Shelley. The man who had defeated the greatest general in history remarked:

53

"I hope to God that I have fought my last battle. It is a bad thing to be always fighting. While in the thick of it I am too much occupied to feel anything, but it is wretched just after . . . . Next to the battle lost, the greatest misery is the battle gained."

The End of the Hundred Days

Napoleon, dull-eyed, ghastly pale, and utterly exhausted, reached Paris by a roundabout route, on June 21. He found the two chambers of the legislature openly hostile. Unwilling to run the risk of igniting a civil war, he signed his second and last abdication, on June 23.

Two days later he withdrew to Malmaison, a hamlet outside Paris, where Empress Josephine had a palace and where she had died just a few months earlier. Josephine had been grossly unfaithful to him, but he had been deeply in love with her at least in the first years of their relationship.

"Poor Josephine," he remarked to Hortense Beauharnais, Josephine's daughter from an earlier marriage, who had accompanied him to her mother's country home. "I can't get used to living here without her. I can still see her coming around a corner to pick the flowers she used to love. Poor Josephine!"

At dawn on June 29, two officials came from Paris, bringing the permission of Joseph Fouché, then president of the provisional government, for Napoleon to leave France. Bonaparte met them in the civilian clothes he had worn since his arrival at Malmaison. As he was discussing the matter with the officials, a column of French infantry marching past shouted, *Vive l'Empereur!*

54

Suddenly the room was in dead silence. From far off came the thuds of cannon as the Prussians advanced on Paris. Napoleon whirled to a wall map in which were stuck pins representing French forces. Rapidly he shifted some pins.

"France will not be governed by a handful of Prussians," Bonaparte declared with his old forcefulness. "I can still check the enemy, and give the government time to negotiate. Then I will sail for the United States and fulfill my destiny there."

He strode out of the room.

A few minutes later he returned in full uniform and sent a dispatch to the provisional government offering himself "not as Emperor but as a general whose name and reputation may still influence the fate of France."

President Fouché refused immediately and emphatically.

About 5:00 that afternoon Napoleon Bonaparte, back in civilian clothes, bid Hortense good-bye, then wandered through the quiet, shadowy rooms of Malmaison for the last time. Outside, a carriage was waiting. Napoleon climbed aboard awkwardly and it rattled off, carrying its pale, brooding occupant away from the dull boom of Prussian cannon and toward the distant sea.

The allies continued to advance upon Paris. The British, who followed the route of the Prussians, were shocked at the trail of destruction and hatred upon which they came, until they became ashamed to be an ally of such a vindictive people. Windows, mirrors, plates, cups were smashed by musket butts or by being hurled against the wall. Tables, chairs, bedposts, desks, picture frames were hacked by sabers. Curtains and blankets were slashed, mattresses ripped open.

"And on the slightest remonstrance of the wretched inhabitants," wrote the British Ensign Gronow, who saw the devastation, "they were beaten in a most shameful manner, and sometimes shot. It is true," he added, "that the Prussians owed the French a long debt of vengeance for all the atrocities committed by the French at Berlin."

On July 8, 1815, Louis XVIII returned to Paris. The prefect of the Seine, the Count de Chambord, greeted the king with a short speech of welcome:

"A hundred days, Sire, have passed since the fateful moment when Your Majesty was forced to quit your capital in the midst of tears . . . ."

Strictly speaking, from March 19 — when Louis fled Paris — to July 8, when he returned, was 111 days. But the count is allowed poetic license. His opening phrase marks a crucial chapter in the life of Napoleon and in France's, Europe's, and the world's long history.

The return of Louis XVIII to Paris after Napoleon's defeat. (The Bettmann Archive)

The Hundred Days and its crowning event, the rout at Waterloo, shattered France's morale, shrank her borders to where they had stood in 1790, undercut the prestige of the Imperial Army — until then considered the greatest fighting machine in Europe — and subjected the proud French people to a humiliation that took them generations to overcome.

After nearly a quarter century of war, France had sacrificed about a million of her sons, with many more crippled for life. Several of her provinces were occupied by allied troops, and she was saddled with a debt of nearly a billion francs in reparations — such were the severe terms imposed by the Second Treaty of Paris, after Waterloo.

Following Napoleon's defeat, patriotism and national unity in Germany, Italy, Russia, Austria, and particularly Great Britain — the nation that always had been the hard core of resistance to Bonaparte — experienced an enormous upsurge.

In Napoleon's career, the Hundred Days serves as a historic microscope to show the growth of his egotism into unrealistic self-glorification and the decline of his formerly acute awareness of the spirit and interests of the French people. As he sagely remarked on his final island of repose, "A man is only a man. His power is nothing if circumstances are not favorable. Opinion is all-important."

Napoleon's actions at Waterloo, and in the period before it, also dramatically demonstrate a loss of the decisiveness he had shown earlier in his military career. Napoleon, at forty-six, was like a champion boxer past his prime, the spring gone out of his legs, his timing off — the result of too many fights, too many victories, too many beatings.

By the end of the Hundred Days, France was on the verge

of civil war. The deep division between the royalists and Bonapartists could not be healed. The government under Louis XVIII adopted repressive measures against Napoleon's followers. A quarter of the army officers and civil servants lost their positions. In a politically rigged trial, Marshal Ney, acclaimed as "the Bravest of the Brave" for his many great victories during the glorious days of the Empire, was tried as a traitor and shot for his role in Bonaparte's return from Elba. The blood of Marshal Ney would prove to be an unwashable stain on the fleur-de-lis of the Bourbons.

Meanwhile, the old regime and many of its conservative trappings had slipped back into the countries of Europe, following the example of Louis XVIII, who had reentered Paris "in the baggage train of the allies." Nonetheless, the forces — of liberalism and nationalism — that were unleashed during the French Revolution and spread throughout the Continent by Napoleon's armies could not be fettered. In the long run, nationalism proved to be the greater force.

In France, two more revolutions — one in 1830 and another in 1848 — would disrupt that nation and bring an end to monarchy there. Napoleon III, a nephew of Napoleon I, would rule France as emperor from 1852 to 1870. After his deposition at the end of the Franco-Prussian War, France would become a republic.

Aftermath

Napoleon reached Rochefort, a seaport on the west coast of France, on July 2, 1815. Two fast frigates were waiting there

Napoleon on board H.M.S. Bellerophon *after his surrender to the English. (National Maritime Museum)*

to speed him across the Atlantic to the United States. The port, however, was blockaded by the British navy.

"Wherever wood can swim," Bonaparte exclaimed, "there I am sure to find this flag of England!"

On July 13, he wrote the prince regent in Great Britain:

"Pursued by the factions which divide my country and by the hostility of the Powers of Europe, I have finished my political career, and I come . . . to sit at the hearth of the British people. I put myself under the protection of the laws which I claim from your Royal Highness as the most powerful, constant and generous of my enemies."

Two days later Napoleon Bonaparte went on board H.M.S. *Bellerophon* and surrendered his sword to her skipper. *Bellerophon* sailed to England, where Napoleon thought he would be put ashore as an exiled guest of the nation. The allies, however, had other plans for him.

He was transferred to H.M.S. *Northumberland* and taken to Saint Helena, the dreary, volcanic island in the South Atlantic on which he would spend the rest of his uneventful days. After being aboard ship for three months, he landed on the dark isle on October 17, 1815.

"Whatever shall we do in that remote spot?" Napoleon remarked as he was being taken into exile. "Well, we shall write our memoirs. Work is the scythe of time."

"There are only two powers in the world," he said. "The sword and the pen. And in the end the former is always conquered by the latter."

Having failed with the sword, Napoleon took up the pen, using the remainder of the short time he had left to build up his legend. He was, according to himself, the champion of equality, liberty, and nationalism, "the natural mediator in this struggle of the past against the Revolution." He also strove to improve upon his military career, emphasizing his successful ventures.

Napoleon died on Saint Helena on May 5, 1821. His last words, spoken in delirium, strangely enough summed up the life, ambition, and loves of this complex, extraordinary man: "France . . . Army . . . Head of the Army . . . Josephine!"

Bibliography

Atteridge, Andrew Hilliard, *The Bravest of the Brave*. New York: Brentano's, 1913.

Aubry, Octave, *The Private Life of Napoleon*. Philadelphia and New York: Lippincott, 1947.

Brett-James, Antony, *The Hundred Days, Napoleon's Last Campaign from Eye-Witness Accounts*. New York: St. Martin's Press, 1964.

De Bertier de Sauvigny, Guillaume, *The Bourbon Restoration*. Translated from the French by Lynn M. Case. Philadelphia: The University of Pennsylvania, 1966.

Delderfield, Ronald F., *Napoleon's Marshals*. Philadelphia and New York: Chilton Company, 1966.

Downey, Fairfax, *Cannonade*. Garden City, New York: Doubleday and Company, Inc., 1966.

Encyclopoedia Britannica. Chicago, London, Toronto: The University of Chicago, 1944.

Gibbs, Montgomery B., *Military Career of Napoleon the Great*. New York: The Saalfield Publishing Company, 1904.

Gottschalk, Louis R., *The Era of the French Revolution*. Boston: Houghton Mifflin, 1929.

Guedalla, Philip, *The Hundred Days*. New York: Grosset & Dunlap, by arrangement with G. P. Putnam's Sons, 1934.

Hayes, Carlton J. H., Baldwin, Marshall Whithed, and Cole, Charles Woolsey, *History of Europe*. New York: The Macmillan Company, 1949.

Headley, J. T., *Napoleon and His Marshals*. New York: Baker and Scribner, 1847.

Herold, J. Christopher, *The Age of Napoleon*. New York: American Heritage Publishing Company, 1963.

Lachouque, Henry, *Napoleon's Battles*. Translated from the French by Roy Monkcom. New York: E. P. Dutton and Company, 1967.

Ludwig, Emil, *Napoleon*. New York: Boni and Liveright, 1926.

Macdonnell, A. G., *Napoleon and His Marshals*. New York: Macmillan, 1934.

McNeill, William H., *The Rise of the West, A History of the Human Community*. Chicago and London: The University of Chicago Press, 1963.

Markham, Felix, *Napoleon*. New York: The New American Library, Inc., 1963.

Sutherland, John, *Men of Waterloo*. Englewood Cliffs, New Jersey: Prentice-Hall, 1966.

Vox, Maximilien, *Napoleon*. New York: Grove Press, Inc., 1960.

Index

Anglo-Dutch army, 28, 39
  numerical strength, 31, 33, 43
  at Quatre Bras, 34, 35, 36, 37
  casualties at Quatre Bras, 37
  retreat from Quatre Bras, 38-39,
    40, 41
  at Waterloo, 43, 46-53
  Waterloo casualties, 52
Angoulême, Duchess of, 23-24
Angoulême, Duke of, 23-25
Aristocracy, French, 23
Armies, allied, 27, 28, 30, 34, 55
  (*see also* Anglo-Dutch army;
    Prussian army)
  casualties of, 37, 38, 52
  numerical strength, 31-33, 43
Army, Grand, 16
  first, lost in Russia, 11
  second, lost at Leipzig, 11-12
  third, surrender of, 12
Army of the North, 27, 30, 33,
    45-46
  in battles at Quatre Bras and
    Ligny, 33-34, 35-37, 44
  casualties at Quatre Bras and
    Ligny, 37, 38
  commanders, 27-28, 33-34
  numerical strength, 27, 31, 43
  at Waterloo, 43, 44, 46-52
  Waterloo casualties, 52
Austria, 13, 25, 26, 57

Battle of the Nations (1813), 12
Beauharnais, Hortense, 54, 55
Belgian troops, 28, 31, 37, 43

Belgium:
  allied armies in, 28-30
  flight of Louis XVIII to, 20
  Napoleon's invasion of, 33
  taken from France, 15
Bellerophon, H.M.S., 60
Berthier, General Louis Alexandre,
    27
Bertrand, Marshal Henri-Gratien,
    14
Blücher, Field Marshal Gebhard,
    33, 34, 35, 44
  army of, 30, 32 (*see also* Prus-
    sian army)
  at Ligny, 37-38
  Waterloo relief troop, 46
Bonaparte, Lucien, 31
Bourbon, House of, 6, 15-16, 19,
    21, 30, 58
British troops, 28, 31, 32, 44, 55
  (*see also* Anglo-Dutch army)
  French opinions of, 44-45
  at Quatre Bras, 36, 37
  at Waterloo, 46-49, 51-53
Brussels, 30, 32, 34

Campbell, Sir Neil, 6, 17
Casualties, 57
  at Quatre Bras and Ligny, 37, 38
  at Waterloo, 52
Caulaincourt, General Armand de,
    13
Chaboulon, Fleury de, 16
Chamber of Deputies, French, 31,
    54

Chambord, Count de, 56
Champ de Mai ceremony, 30-31
Charleroi, 30, 32, 33, 34
Chateaubriand, Viscount de, 25
Clausel, Marshal Bertrand, 24
Code Napoléon, 8
Congress of Vienna, 13, 16, 26
Constitutional monarchy, 15, 23, 30
Continental blockade, 10

De Reille, General H. C., 44-45
Dutch troops, 28, 31, 37, 43. *See also* Anglo-Dutch army

Elba, 12, 14
  Napoleon's escape from, 3-6, 17, 26
  Napoleon's exile, 12-17, 39
Europe:
  Congress of Vienna, 16, 26
  in Napoleonic era, 10, 14
  post-Napoleonic, 57, 58

Fouché, Joseph, 25-26, 54-55
France:
  attitudes toward Napoleon, 6-8, 13, 16, 18-19, 21-26, 28, 54
  civil liberties, 8, 15, 30
  Constitution of 1815, 30
  as constitutional monarchy, 15, 23, 30
  as a dictatorship, 10, 30
  under Louis XVIII, 12, 15-16, 59
  under Napoleon, 8-10, 15, 30
  Napoleon's return to, 6, 17-23

republic, 58
revolutions of 1830 and 1848, 58
second Empire, 58
after Waterloo, 54, 56-58
Francis, Emperor of Austria, 13
Franco-Prussian War, 58
French army, 27 (*see also* Army, Grand; Army of the North; Imperial Guard)
  deserts Louis XVIII for Napoleon, 6-8, 18-20, 24
  losses of Napoleonic War, 57
French Revolution, 8, 15, 23, 30, 58

German troops. *See* Prussian army
Germany, rise of nationalism, 10, 57
Ghent, Louis XVIII at, 41
Grant, Colonel Colquhuon, 34
Great Britain, 13, 26, 57, 58-60 (*see also* British troops)
  blockade of, 10
Grenoble, 6, 8, 17
Gronow, Rees Howell, 49, 56
Grouchy, Marshal Emmanuel de, 28, 39, 40, 43, 44

Heymes, Colonel, 50
Hugo, Victor, 42

Imperial Guard, 4, 14, 37, 39
  at Waterloo, 50, 51-52
Inconstant, the, 3, 4
Italy, rise of nationalism, 10, 57

Josephine, Empress, 13, 54, 60

La Bedoyère, Colonel François, 30
La Belle Alliance, 41, 42-45, 46, 48
Laffray Pass, Napoleon at, 6-8
Lanjuinais, Count Jean-Denis, 31
Lavalette, Count, 22
Leipzig, Battle of, 12
Les Miserables (Hugo), 42
Ligny, 33, 35
  battle at, 37-38, 39, 44
Louis XVI, King, 12, 23
Louis XVIII, King, 4, 12, 15-16, 18-21, 23, 58
  at Ghent, 41
  leaves Paris, 20-21
  returns to Paris, 56, 58

Maitland, Sir Peregrine, 51
Malmaison, Napoleon at, 54-55
Marie Antoinette, Queen, 23
Marie-Louise, Empress, 13
Marmont, Marshal Auguste Frederic, 20
Metternich, Prince von, 13
Mont St. Jean, 38, 39, 40, 41, 43, 44, 48, 52
Montélimar, 25
Murat, Joachim, King of Naples, 27

Napoleon Bonaparte:
  abdication of (1814), 12
  abdication of (1815), 54
  army and commanders of, 27-28
    (*see also* Army of the North)
  in Battle of Waterloo, 44, 46, 50-52, 57
  birth date and place, 14
  death of, 60
  his earlier warfare, 10-12
  as emperor, 10-12, 15
  escape from Elba, 3-6, 17, 26
  exile at Elba, 12-17, 39
  exile at Saint Helena, 60
  leaves France (1815), 55, 58-59
  lost twelve hours, 39
  marriages of, 13
  military tactics of, 41, 42-45
  his opinion of Wellington, 44
  personal decline of, 57
  physical appearance of, 39
  his plan of action against allied armies, 28-30, 33-34, 35, 39, 40, 41
  at Quatre Bras and Ligny, 33-38, 39
  return to France (1815), 6, 17-23
  rise to power, 8-10
  son of, 13
  suicide attempt of, 13
Napoleon Francis, King of Rome, 13, 16
Napoleon III, Emperor, 58
Nationalism, rise of, 10, 57, 58
Ney, Marshal Michel, 19, 20, 28, 39
  given command, 33-34
  at Quatre Bras, 35-37
  trial and death of, 58
  at Waterloo, 43, 46, 48-52
Northumberland, H. M. S., 60

65

Oudinot, Eugenie, 18
Oudinot, Marshal Nicholas-
   Charles, 18-19, 27

Paris:
   abandoned by Louis XVIII, 21
   allied objective, 27, 28, 55
   arrival of Napoleon in, 22-23
   return of Louis XVIII to, 56, 58
   surrender of (1814), 12
Paris, Treaty of. *See* Treaty
Peninsular War, 32, 44, 45
Prussia, 13, 26
Prussian army, 30, 32, 34, 39
   advance on Paris, 55-56
   in battle at Ligny, 35, 36, 37-38
   casualties at Ligny, 38
   one Corps requested by Welling-
      ton, 38, 46
   desertions from, 38
   between Ligny and Waterloo,
      38, 40, 41, 44
   numerical strength, 32
   at Waterloo, 46, 51, 52
   Waterloo casualties, 52

Quatre Bras, 30, 38-39
   battle at, 34, 35-37, 39, 44

Richmond, Duchess of, 34-35
Rome, King of. *See* Napoleon
   Francis
Royalists, French, 19-20, 23-26,
   58

Russia, 13, 26, 57
   Napoleon's campaign in, 11

Saint Helena, 16, 60
Shelley, Frances, Lady, 53
Soult, Marshal Nicholas, 28, 44

"Telegraph," 17-18
Treaty of Paris:
   of 1814, 12, 14-15, 16, 26
   of 1815, 57

Undaunted, H. M. S., 13
Uxbridge, Lord, 40-41, 46

Valence, 25
Vienna, Congress of, 13, 16, 26
Vitrolles, Baron Eugène François
   de, 23, 25

Waldie, Charlotte, 34-35
Wars, Napoleonic, 10-12, 57
Waterloo, 30, 38, 40
   Battle of, 44-53, 57
Wavre, 38, 40
Wellington, Duke of, 33, 34-35,
   43, 44
   army of, 28, 31-33
   at Quatre Bras, 37, 38
   quoted, 32, 33, 52-54
   request for Prussian relief corps,
      38, 46
   at Waterloo, 40-41, 46, 49, 51-
      53